THE PLANT

and its

Ornamental applications

THE PLANT

and its

Ornamental applications

UNDER THE DIRECTION

OF

Mr. Eugène GRASSET

Original Edition

PARIS

LIBRAIRIE CENTRALE DES BEAUX-ARTS

E. LEVY, Éditeur

13, rue Lafayette.

Adaptation, translation and layout

Thomas PEETERS

Table of contents

A word about the author

Eugène Grasset (1845-1917) is one of the most influential figures of Art Nouveau, an artistic movement that began at the end of the 19th century. Born in Switzerland, Grasset left an indelible mark on the world of art, design and decoration thanks to his exceptional talent and avant-garde vision.

Grasset began his career as an apprentice sculptor in Zurich before moving to Paris, where he quickly gained recognition for his innovative creations. His work is characterized by a deep fascination with nature and an ability to capture the complex beauty of organic forms.

One of Grasset's most celebrated achievements is his crucial influence in the formation of Art Nouveau. He made a significant contribution to the aesthetics of the movement, creating mesmerizing floral motifs and nature-inspired ornaments that have become emblematic of this artistic period. His posters, jewelry, furniture and illustrations caused a sensation across Europe, helping to redefine standards of beauty and decoration.

In addition to his artistic work, Grasset also shared his expertise as a teacher at the École Guérin in Paris, where he trained many artists and designers who would in turn leave their mark on the world of art and design.

"La plante et ses applications ornementales" is a significant work by Grasset. In this book, he demonstrates how botanical elements can be harmoniously incorporated into artistic creations. It's a work that continues to inspire designers around the world.

INTRODUCTION

For a long time now, artists, critics and connoisseurs - some sincerely, others slyly hypocritical - have been demanding that we stop copying dead centuries that no longer have anything to say to us.

The artificial sap that sustained the arts, sons of the Renaissance, has long since ceased to flow, and what remains of them in Europe is no more than a stammering.

When artists are rightly criticized for being "old-fashioned" and endlessly rehashing the worn-out, meaningless formulas of the past, they never fail to attribute to their opponents the exorbitant pretension of demanding something fundamentally new. - Everyone knows that new simply means to improve, to make progress.

We therefore have no pretension of inventing an Art, which is impossible, and we shall be content to try to move forward, abandoning all copying of the ornaments of another age.

But nothing can be founded on nothing, and anyone wishing to work in a sound manner must possess a method based both on reasoning and on the age-old experience of past eras; but in no case on copying the objects left by those eras, as is done so flatly, so poorly, so shabbily today.

III

Today's craftsmen need to place themselves in the state of archaeological ignorance of the workers of yesteryear, who looked at beautiful things, but didn't calk them. Tradition was perpetuated, modified with each generation.

Now, since the end of the last century, there is no longer any tradition that we can continue or rely on, so we'd better get back to the reasoned origins of Art, taking constructive needs as the basis of composition, and adopting ornamentation borrowed from nature.

But these natural forms can only be used if they are modified to fit closely with the material from which they are made. It's by ignoring this simple and healthy truth that all styles have fallen into decadence; for there have always been "clever" people who wanted to make things more natural than they were; it's for this reason that moderns have been floundering for so long, without knowing why they are struck by impotence.

For many years now, I have dedicated myself to the very interesting task of attempting this return to the original source, and I have tried to communicate my hope to young minds not yet ankylosed to the sterile decals of the past, but who nevertheless know how to look, full of respect and with fruit, at what was the glory of mankind.

Far from claiming to be a masterpiece, we shall be content to show industry, above all, practical examples and a path to follow; but we shall give no rest to the very principle that guides us, the implacable war on imitation of the past.

The task is a difficult one, since almost everything remains to be done, and we cannot, as our ancient predecessors did, I repeat, rely on the inventions of our immediate fathers.

For my part, I go into battle confident of success, accompanied by a modest phalanx of young people;

a fresh troupe, to say the least, as its ranks are growing daily with the arrival of many young girls and they are not the least valiant today, as life has become hard for everyone, and the sense of duty, often blunted or absent in the stronger sex, is replaced in this case by the most abominable vanity, to the point where the name "ornamentalist", for some young men, has become at least as seriously insulting as that of "surveyor".

There are no secrets or procedures in the models in this book. On the contrary, every example is supported by a plate drawn from life with the most rigorous accuracy, and anyone who compares the study with the interpretation can try to do the same according to his or her personal feeling. Indeed, although this publication provides over one hundred and fifty ready-to-use motifs, the number can be increased indefinitely by analogy.

Such a collection could not do without color; for if drawing is the decision of the materialized idea, color is its visible sensibility.

But far be it for grey, ash grey, grave grey, impotent grey, "decorative" grey in a word! If we're talking about color, we're talking about real color, with its full keyboard. Because it's also time to restore this all-powerful element of effect, now so misunderstood, so contaminated, so barbarously employed: anaemia reigns over the ruins of past imitation. We're going to regain new strength through contact with nature; we're going to draw from it, with our independence finally regained, a new, rich and generous blood.

It is no longer empty words, always easy to find, that we bring here, but, what is less easy, deeds.

Eugène GRASSET.

April 1896.

IRIS IRIS Die SCHWERT LILIE

IRIS   IRIS   Die SCHWERT LILIE

IRIS   IRIS   Die Schwert Lilie

POPPY   PAVOT   Der MOHN

POPPY   PAVOT   Der MOHN

POPPY   PAVOT   Der MOHN

Water-Lily   Nenuphar   Die See Rose

WATER·LILY   NENUPHAR   Die SEE ROSE

Water-Lily   Nenuphar   Die See Rose

COLUMBINE   ANCOLIE   Die AGLEI

COLUMBINE   ANCOLIE   Die AGLEI

COLUMBINE   ANCOLIE   Die AGLEI

COURD   COURGE   Der Kürbiss

COURD COURGE Der KÜRBISS

COURD   COURGE   Der KÜRBISS

CROWN IMPERIAL   COURONNE IMPERIALE   Die NEBENKRONE

Crown Imperial　　Couronne Imperiale　　Die Nebenkrone

CROWN IMPERIAL   COURONNE IMPERIALE   Die NEBENKRONE

Pl.19.
J.Milesi
GERANIUM
GERANIUM SAUVAGE
Das GERANIUM

GERANIUM

GERANIUM SAUVGE

Das GERANIUM

GERANIUM   GERANIUM SAUVGE   Das GERANIUM

CYCLAMEN   CYCLAMEN   Die ERDSCHEIBE

Cyclamen   Cyclamen   Die Erdscheibe

CYCLAMEN   CYCLAMEN   Die ERDSCHEIBE

ARROW-HEAD   SAGITTAIRE   Das PFEILKRAUT

ARROW-HEAD

SAGITTAIRE

Das PFEILKRAUT

Arrow-head   Sagittaire   Das Pfeilkraut

Jonquil   Jonquille   Die Jonquille

JONQUIL   JONQUILLE   Die JONQUILLE

JONQUIL   JONQUILLE   Die JONQUILLE

SNOWDROP   PERCE-NEIGE   Das SCHNEE-GLÖCKCHEN

SNOWDROP   PERCE-NEIGE   Das SCHNEE-GLÖCKCHEN

SNOWDROP   PERCE-NEIGE   Das SCHNEE-GLÖCKCHEN

SOLOMON'S SEAL   SCEAU DE SALOMON   Der SALOMONS SIEGEL

SOLOMON'S SEAL   SCEAU DE SALOMON   Der SALOMONS SIEGEL

SOLOMON'S SEAL   SCEAU DE SALOMON   Der SALOMONS SIEGEL

LILY OF THE VALLEY   MUGUET   Die MAIBLUME

LILY OF THE VALLEY   MUGUET   Die MAIBLUME

LILY OF THE VALLEY   MUGUET   Die MAIBLUME

NASTURTIUM CAPUCINE Die MAIBLUME

NASTURTIUM   CAPUCINE   Die KAPUZINERKREFFE

NASTURTIUM   CAPUCINE   Die KAPUZINERKREFFE

DANDELION

PISSENLIT

Der LÖWENZAHN

DANDELION   PISSENLIT   Der LÖWENZAHN

DANDELION   PISSENLIT   Der LÖWENZAHN

GLYCINE　　　　　GLYCINE　　　　　Die BOHRBLUME

GLYCINE

GLYCINE

Die BOHRBLUME

ADIDEVIN

GLYCINE

GLYCINE

DIE BOHRBLUME

LILAC   LILAS   Das LILA

LILAC   LILAS   DAS LILA

LILAC   LILAS   DAS LILA

CHESTNUT - TREE — MARRONNIER — Der KASTANIENBAUM

CHESTNUT-TREE   MARRONNIER   Der KASTANIENBAUM

CHESTNUT - TREE   MARRONNIER   Der KASTANIENBAUM

MONKS HOOD   ACONIT   Der EISENHUT

MONKS HOOD   ACONIT   Der EISENHUT

MONKS HOOD   ACONIT   Der EISENHUT

THISTLE — CHARDON — Die DISTEL

THISTLE   CHARDON   Die DISTEL

THISTLE CHARDON Die DISTEL

Pl 61
Marcelle GAUDIN
PERIWINKLE
PERVENCHE
Das SINNGRÜNN

PERIWINKLE   PERVENCHE   Das SINNGRÖNN

PERIWINKLE.   PERVENCHE.   Das SINNGRÖNN

BUTTER-CUP

BOUTON D'OR

Die GOLDBLUME

BUTTER-CUP BOUTON D'OR Die GOLDBLUME

BUTTER-CUP   BOUTON D'OR   Die GOLDBLUME

WILD ROSE   EGLANTIER   Die WILDE ROSE

WILD ROSE   EGLANTIER   Die WILDE ROSE

WILD ROSE   EGLANTIER   Die WILDE ROSE

CHRYSANTHEMUM   CHRYSANTHÈME   Das CHRYSANTHEMUM

CHRYSANTHEMUM   CHRYSANTHÈME   Das CHRYSANTHEMUM

Chrysanthemum   Chrysanthème   Das Chrysanthemum